GW01312783

This book belongs to:

..........Thea..

scan this code:

All mushrooms are fungi, but mushrooms are not like mildew or other types of fungi. Mushrooms belong to the kingdom of Fungi.

A number of fungi species:
There are over 6 million species of fungi in the world.

A number of mushroom species:
Approximately 14,000 species

Mushrooms derive nutrients from food sources in their environment, such as animal waste, plant matter, and organic carbon.

The mushrooms we eat are generally composed of a stipe (stem), a pileus (cap), and lamellae (gills).

Mushroom vs Fungi:

The difference between mushrooms and fungus is that the mushrooms are fruiting bodies of certain fungi while the fungus is any member of microorganisms such as yeast, molds, mildews, mushrooms, etc., that belong to Kingdom Fungi.

Fact 1: In nature, some species of mushrooms may have a body that spreads over hundreds of square miles.

BOLETE

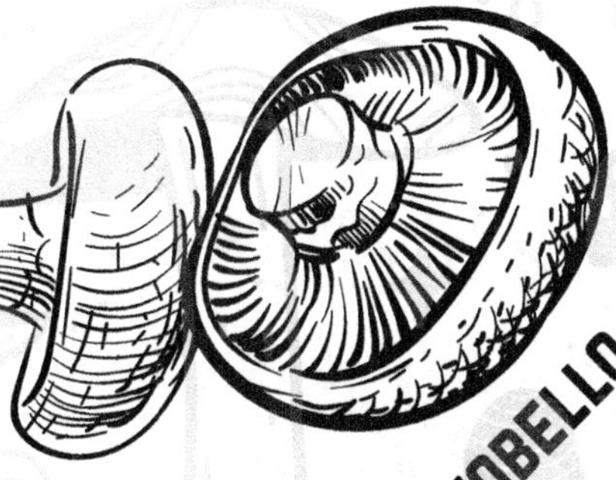

PORTOBELLO

Fact 2: Mushrooms are genetically closer to humans than plants.

CHANTERELLE

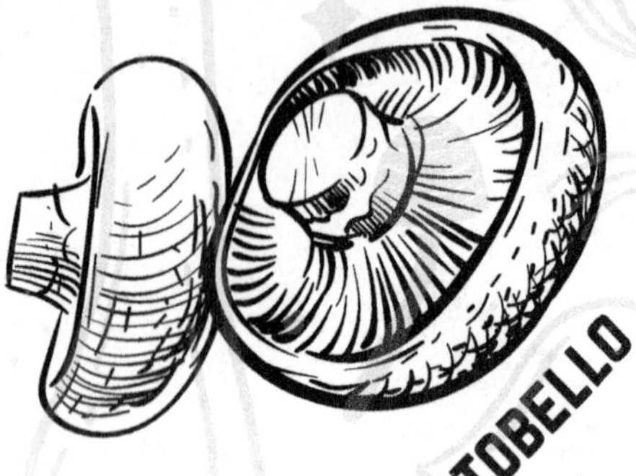

PORTOBELLO

Fact 3: Mushrooms contain a pro-vitamin which is converted to vitamin D when exposed to the sun.

BOLETE

CHANTERELLE

Fact 4: Mushrooms are made up of 90 percent water.

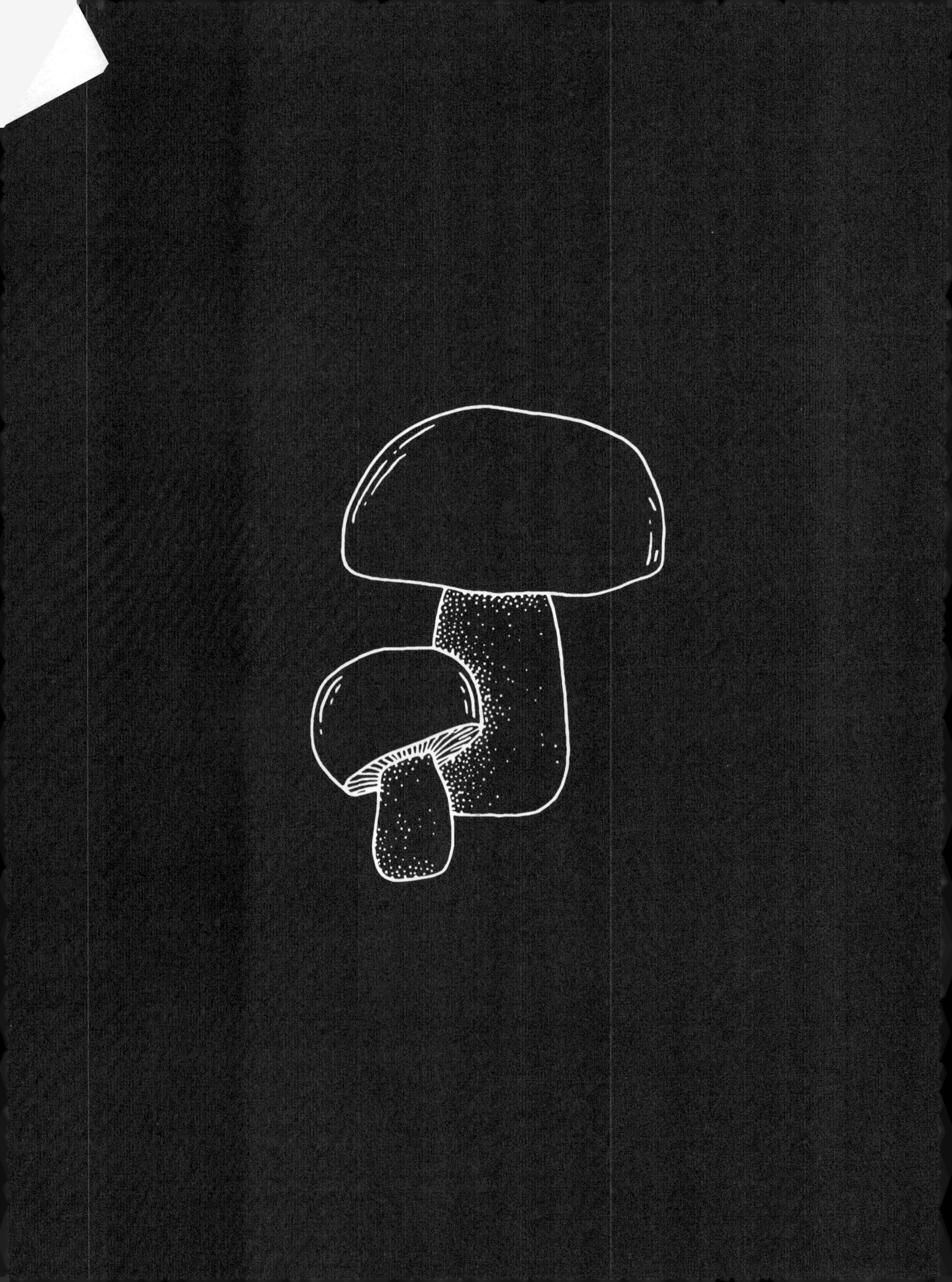

KING TRUMPET

Fact 5: Traditional Chinese medicine uses mushrooms for their medicinal properties.

CHAMPIGNON

Fact 6: In Ancient Egypt mushrooms were considered to be exclusively for royalty.

SHIMEJI

KING TRUMPET

SHIMEJI

Fact 7: There are over 75 species of mushrooms that glow in the dark.

Fact 8: The largest part of the fungus is the underground network of mycelium, the primary role of mycelium is to reproduce and ensure the survival of its species.

CHAMPIGNON

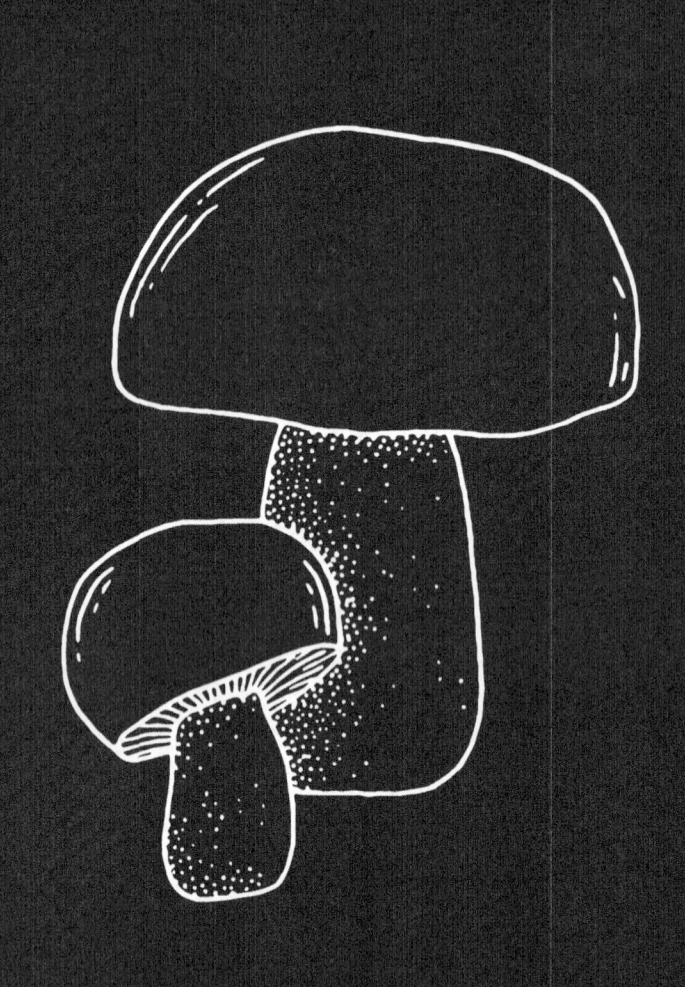

OYSTER MUSHROOMS

ENOKI

NISCALO

Fact 9: Mushrooms can stay dormant for years.

Fact 10: Mushrooms make colorful natural dyes. You can produce almost any color imaginable using different combinations of mushrooms and solvents.

Fact 11: Mushrooms are low energy dense low in calories, fat-free, cholesterol-free and gluten-free.

NISCALO

ENOKI

OYSTER MUSHROOMS

Fact 12: There are 2189 edible mushrooms. Of these, 1006 are safe to eat, and 183 need pre-treatment to make them safe to eat.

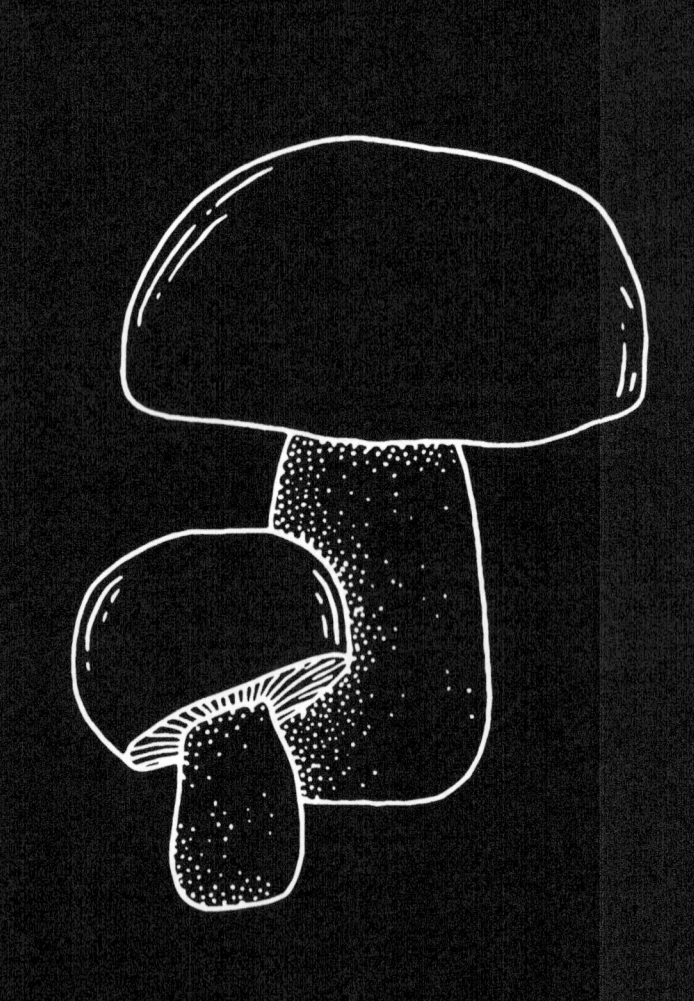

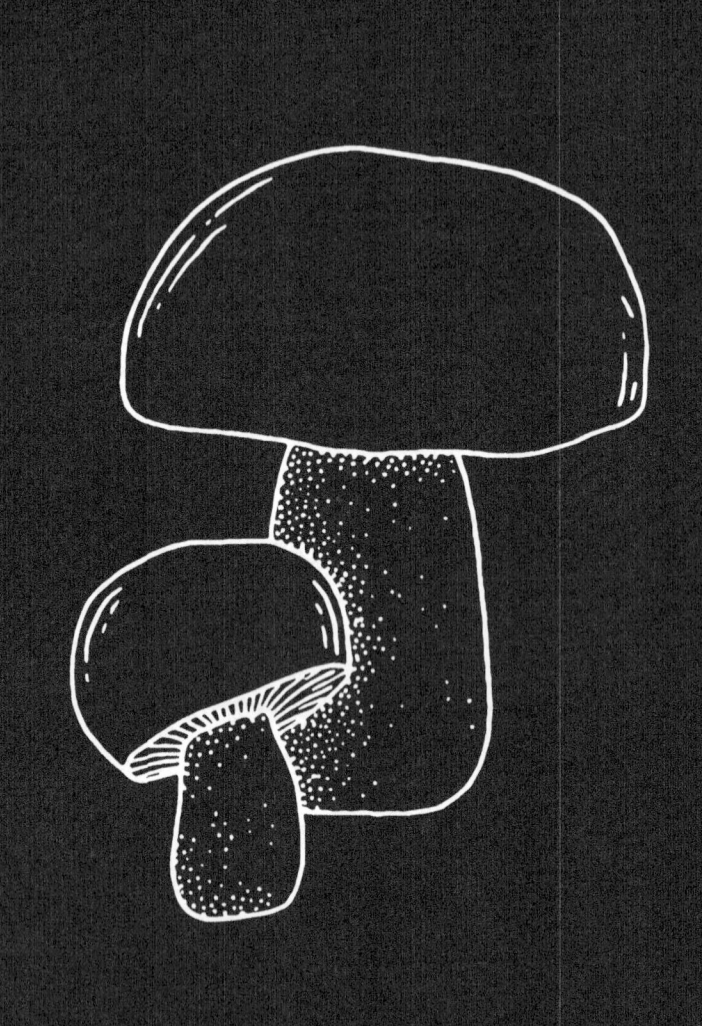

Fact 13: Yartsa Gunbu is the most expensive edible mushroom in the world.

Fact 14: Mushrooms can turn plastic into the food. More than 50 types of mushrooms have been discovered that can digest and break down different types of plastics.

Fact 15: Approximately 50 percent of all known mushrooms are inedible but harmless, 20 percent can make you sick, and one percent could kill you.

Fact 16: Mushrooms create Fairy Rings. They are naturally occurring circles of mushrooms that appear year after year in grassy areas and woodlands.

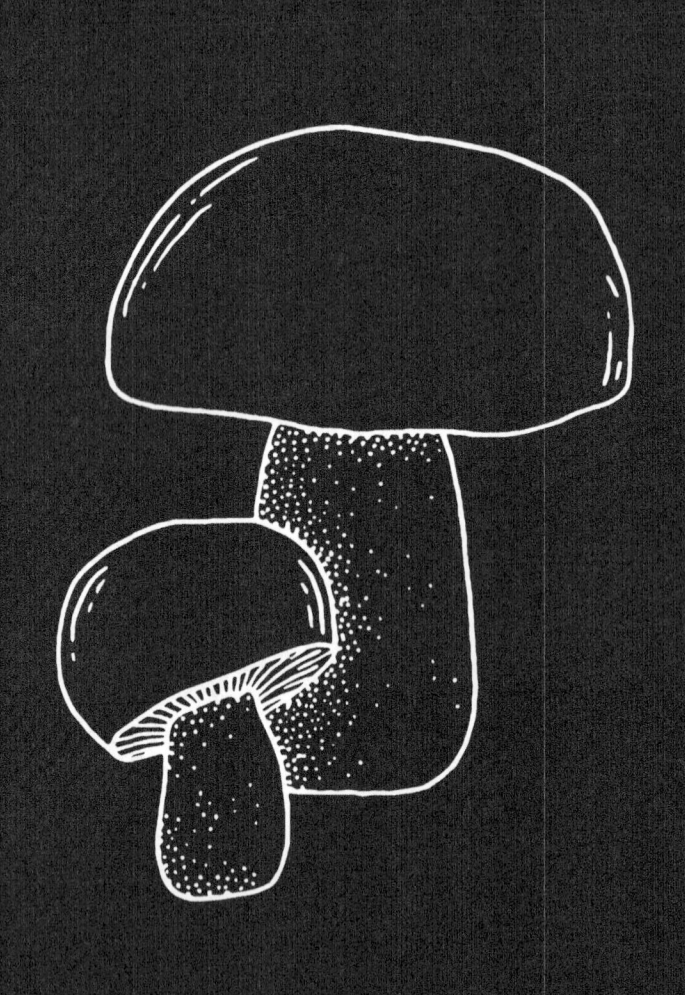

Fact 17: More than 350 million years ago, towering mushrooms 24 ft (7.3 m) tall and 3 ft (90 cm) wide dotted the landscape.

Fact 18: In 1991 hikers found a 5,300-year-old, mummified body in a melting glacier in the Italian Alps. He carried two different types of mushrooms with him.

Fact 19. It takes less water, energy and space to produce a kilogram of mushrooms than to produce other foods.

Fact 20. Some species of wild mushrooms can grow from pins to full-grown mushrooms in less than a day.

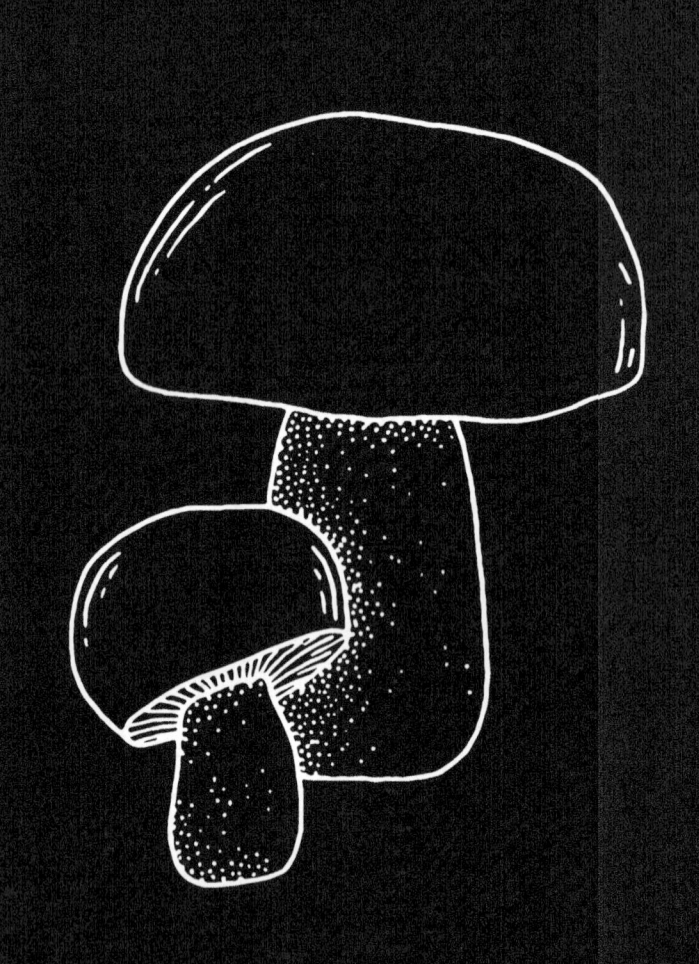

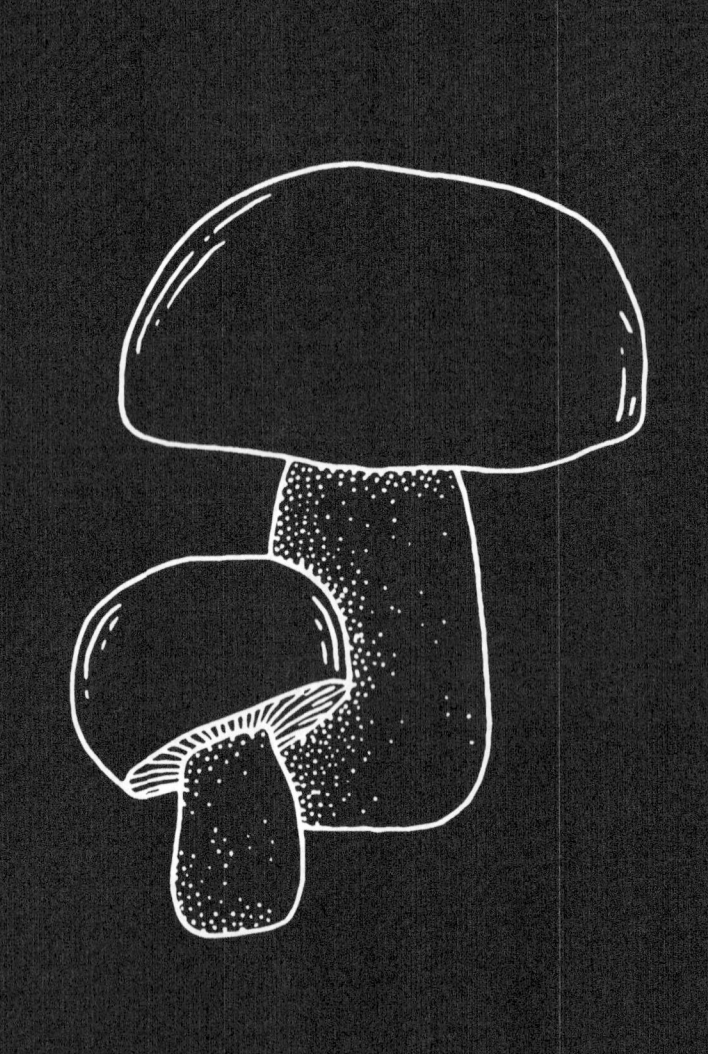

Fact 21: There is a 2400-year-old giant "honey mushroom" in US' Oregon, covering 2,200 acres, slowly killing off the trees in the forest. It is the largest living organism on the planet.

Fact 22: Some mushrooms can actually generate their own wind, pushing themselves up to four inches up and sideways.

Fact 23. There is an entire species of mushrooms, found all over the world, that tastes like fried chicken. It's even referred to as the "chicken of the woods."

Fact 24. Most medium to large mushroom species take three to four days to reach maturity.

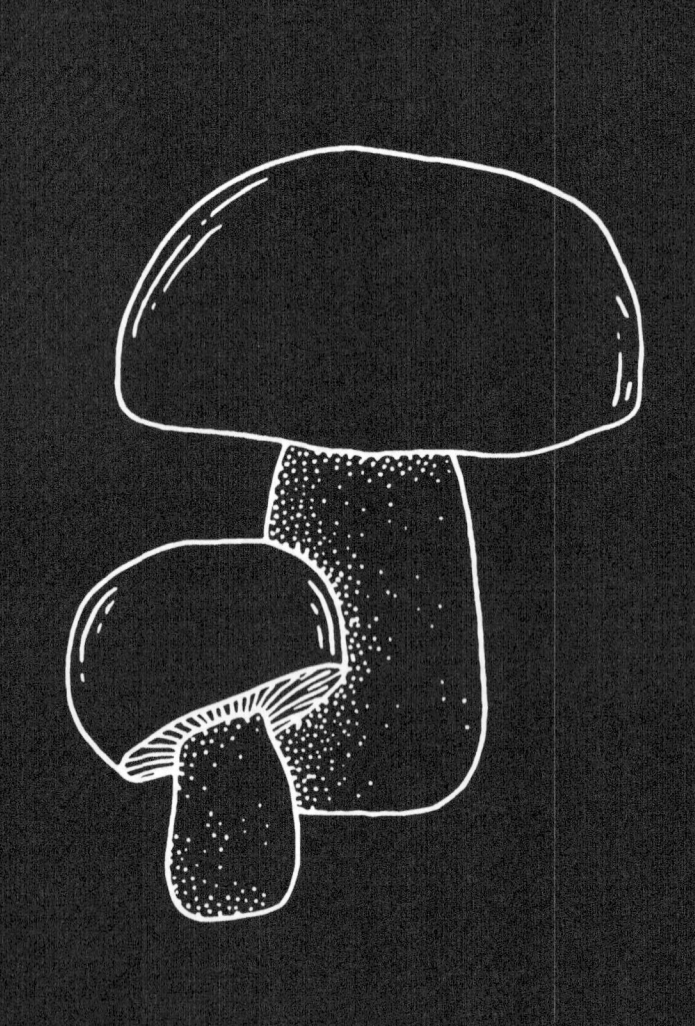

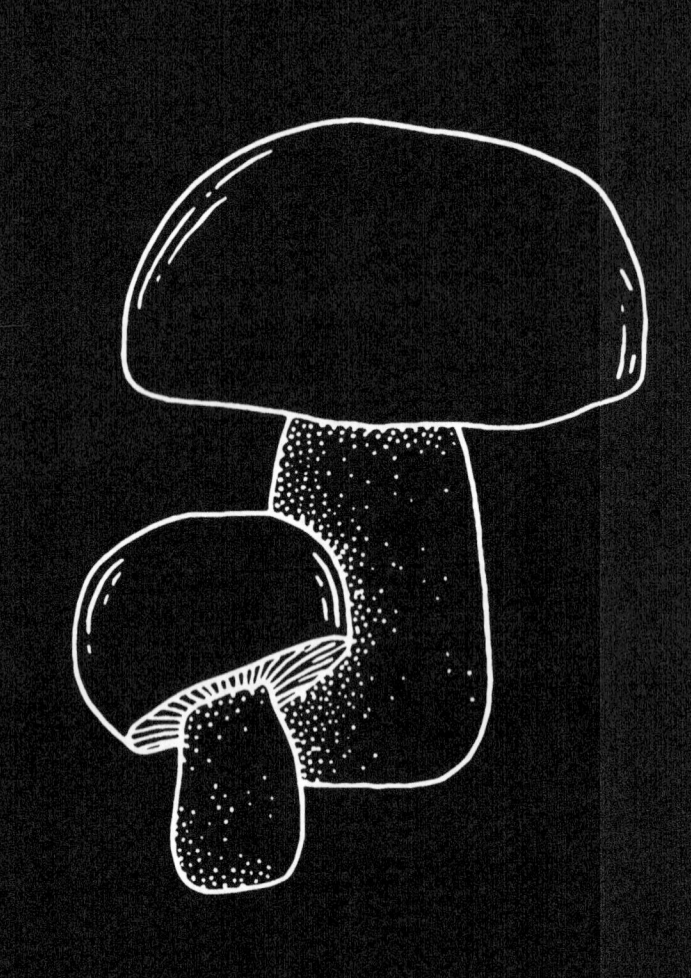

Fact 25: Amanita phalloides is the deadliest mushroom there is. It is responsible for the majority of fatal mushroom poisonings worldwide.

Fact 26: Much of the spooky old lore about ghosts and bog lights is now known to be simply mushrooms glowing in the dark.

Fact 27: Santa was once a mushroom! Early Arctic shamans celebrated the winter solstice by dressing in red and white, and giving the mushroom Amanita muscaria as gifts. Shamans would drop these gifts down the open top of their neighbor's teepee.

Fact 28: 350 million years ago, there existed a 20-foot-tall mushroom in Saudi Arabia. It was likely the largest living thing on dry land at that time.

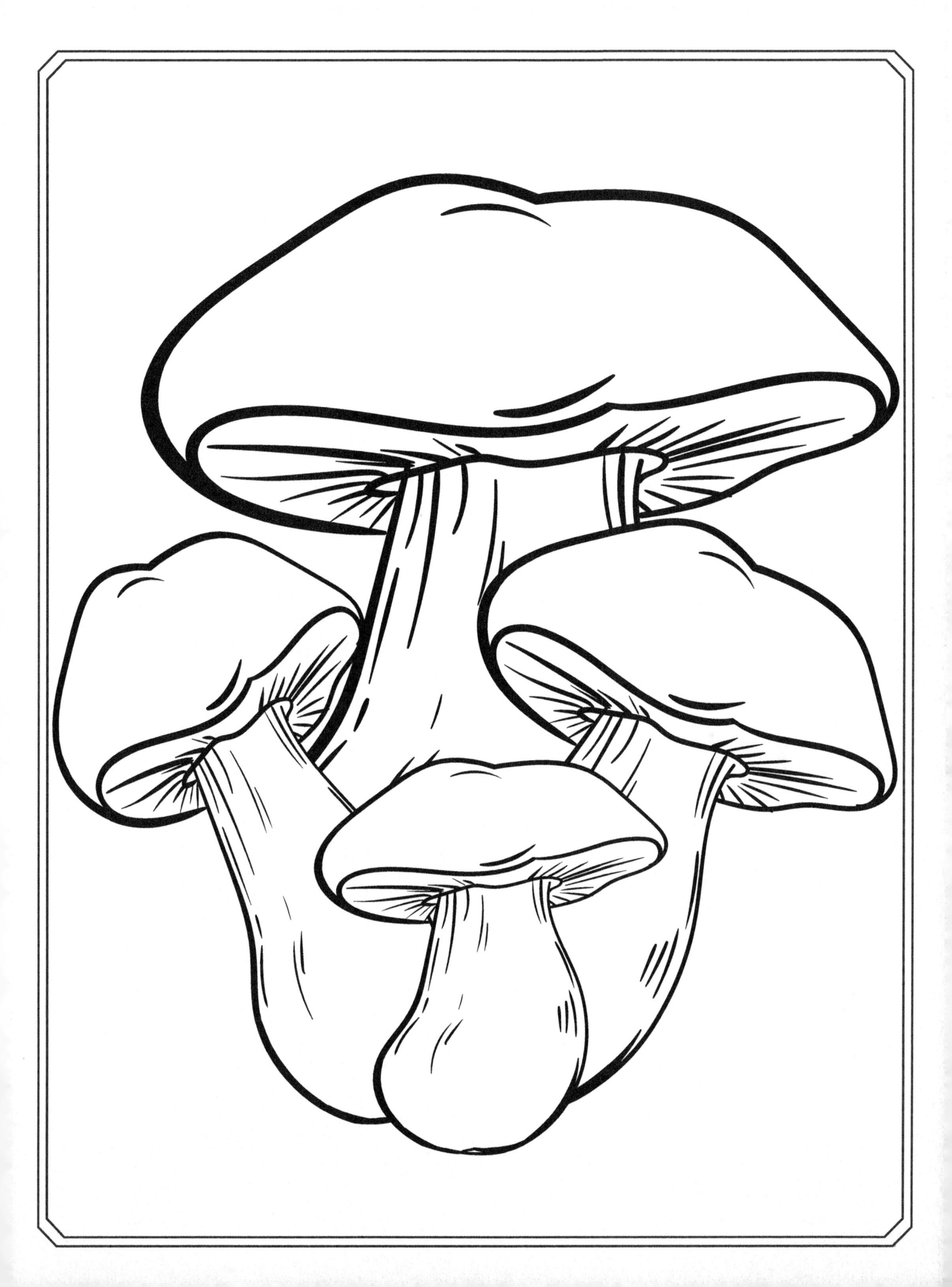

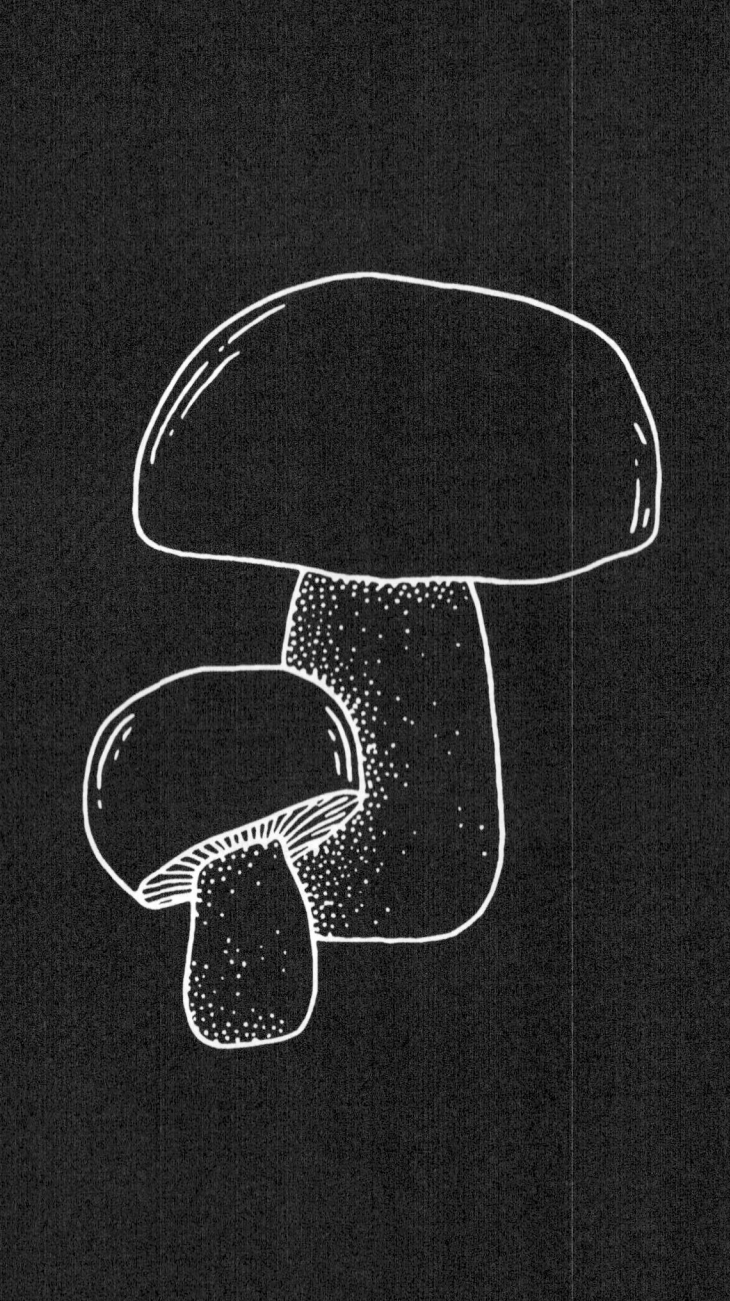

Fact 29: Fly Agaric mushrooms, which look like Super Mario mushrooms, contain a psychoactive chemical that can cause the illusion that objects around you are larger or smaller than they actually are.

Fact 30: Reindeers love to eat psychedelic mushrooms.

Fact 31: There is a mushroom that looks like a brain and is so dangerous to eat that Switzerland and Germany prohibit it to be sold.

Fact 32: The most expensive single food ingredient sold was a 3.3lb white truffle, a subterranean mushroom that sold for $330,000.

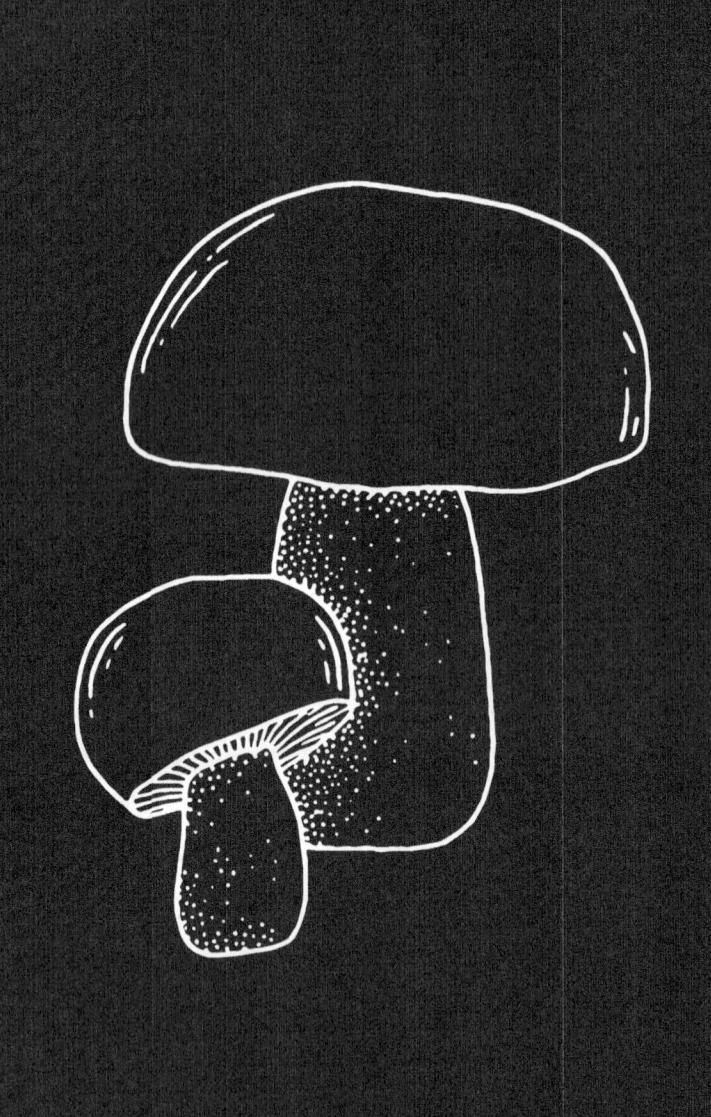

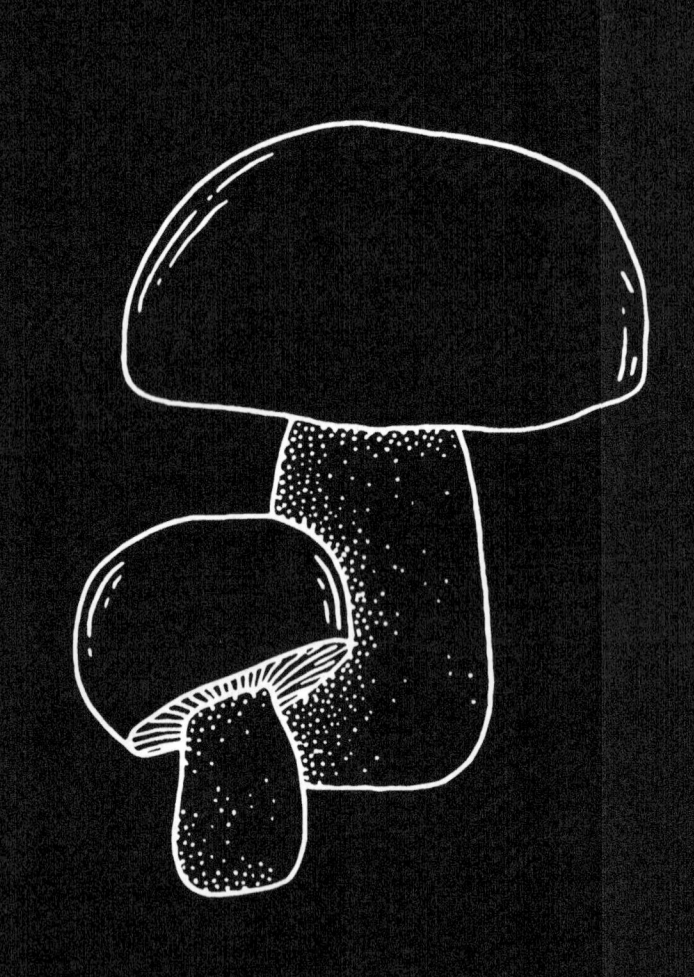

Fact 33: There is a mushroom that dissolves itself. It is edible, but it must be cooked or eaten within hours of picking.

Fact 34: Mushrooms can be useful for antibacterial, anti-inflammatories and antioxidants. While also helping to reduce blood pressure, moderate blood sugar, reduce cholesterol.

Fact 35: A single Portabella mushroom can contain more potassium than a banana.

Fact 36: The mushroom is used in many cuisines throughout the world and it is known as the "meat" of the vegetable world.

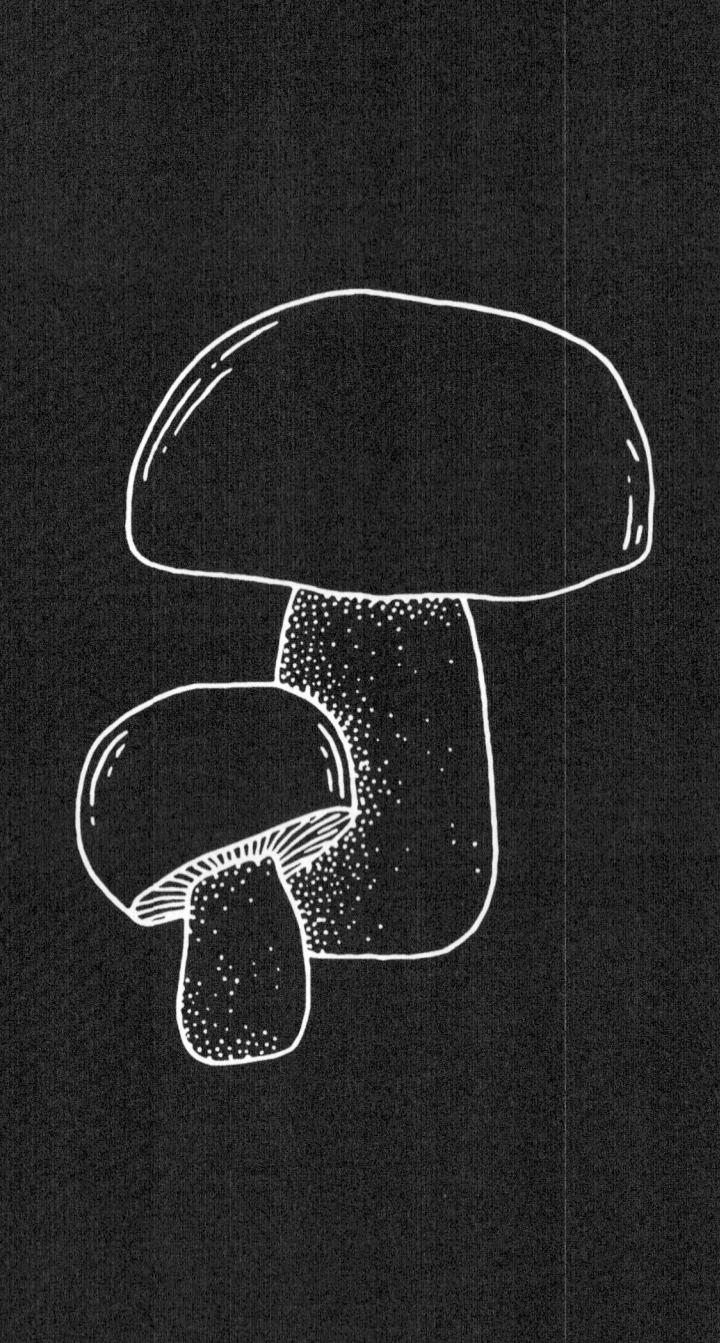

Fact 37: The most popular type representing 90% of mushrooms consumed in the US is the white button mushroom.

Fact 38: The world's largest producer of edible mushrooms is China which produces about half of all cultivated mushrooms.

Fact 39: Before the invention of synthetic dyes, mushrooms were widely used for dyeing wool and other natural fibers.

Fact 40: The act of collecting these mushrooms is known as 'mushroom hunting', or 'mushrooming'.

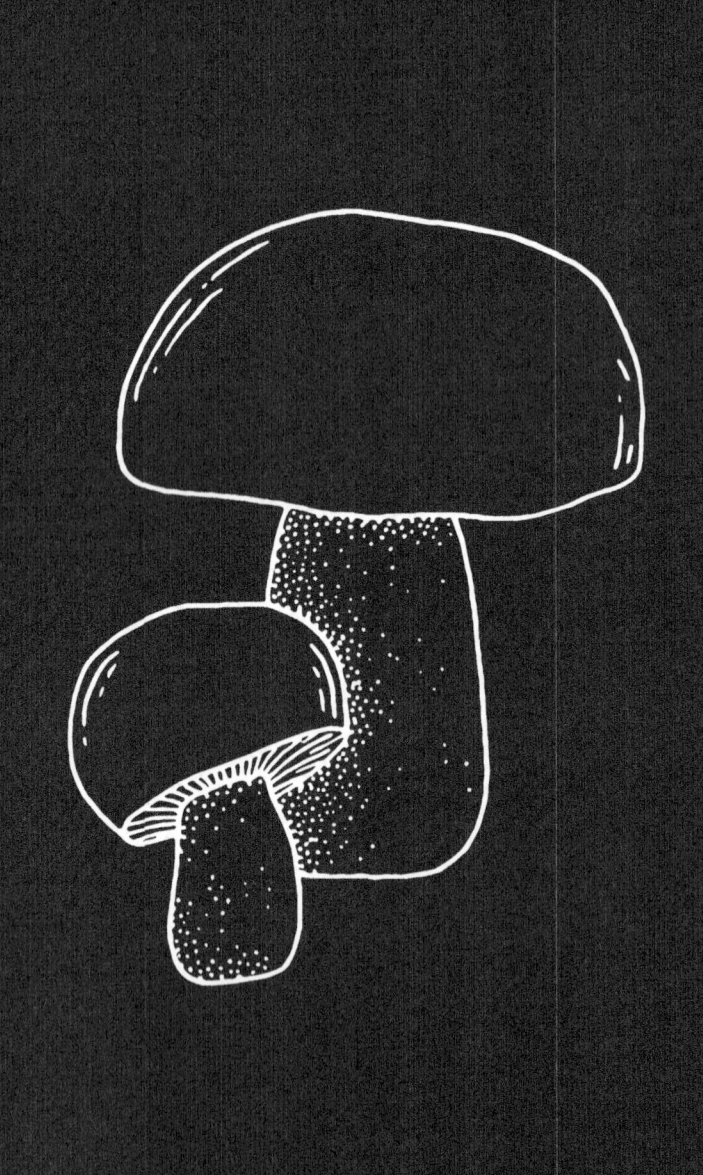

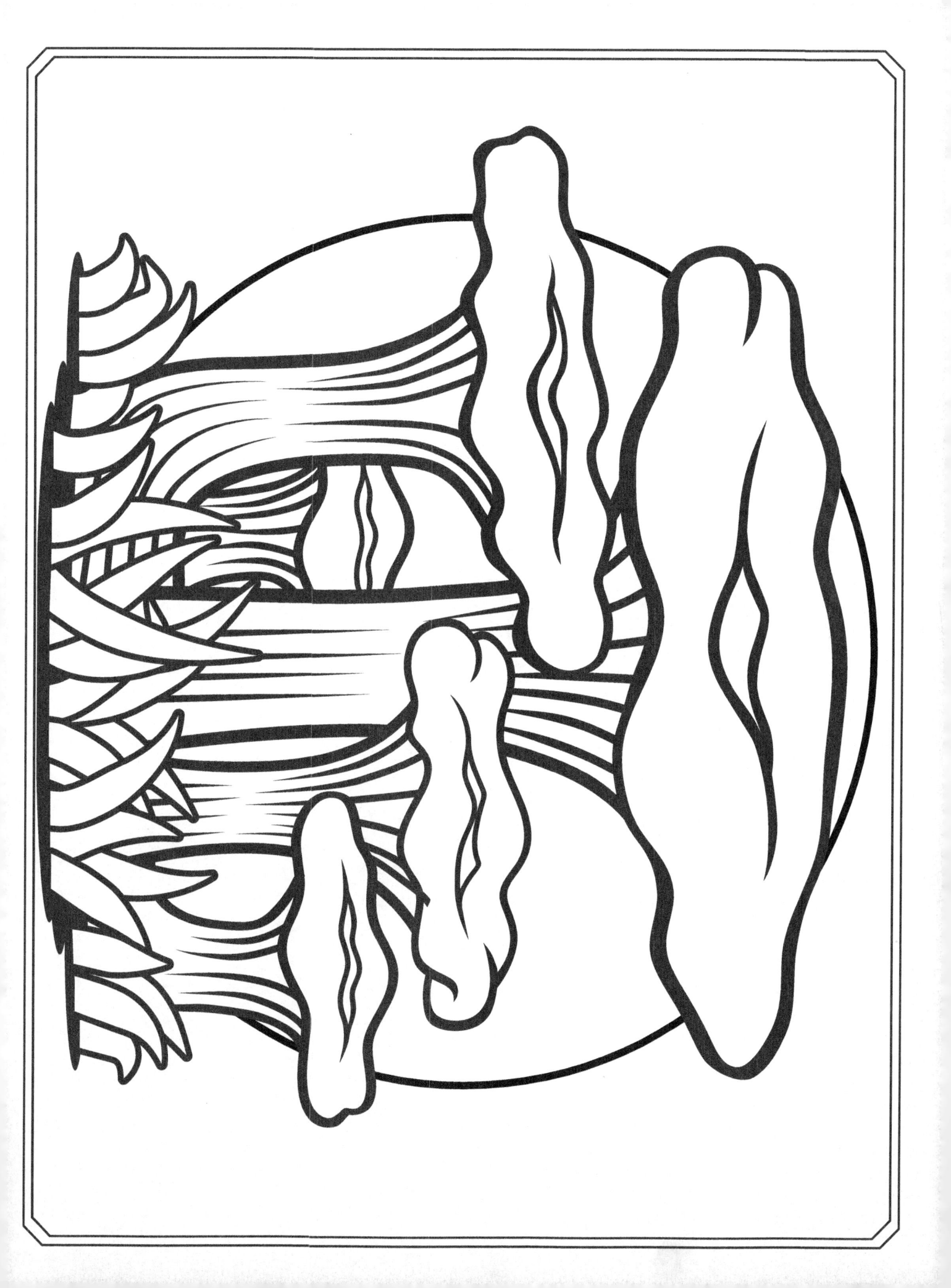

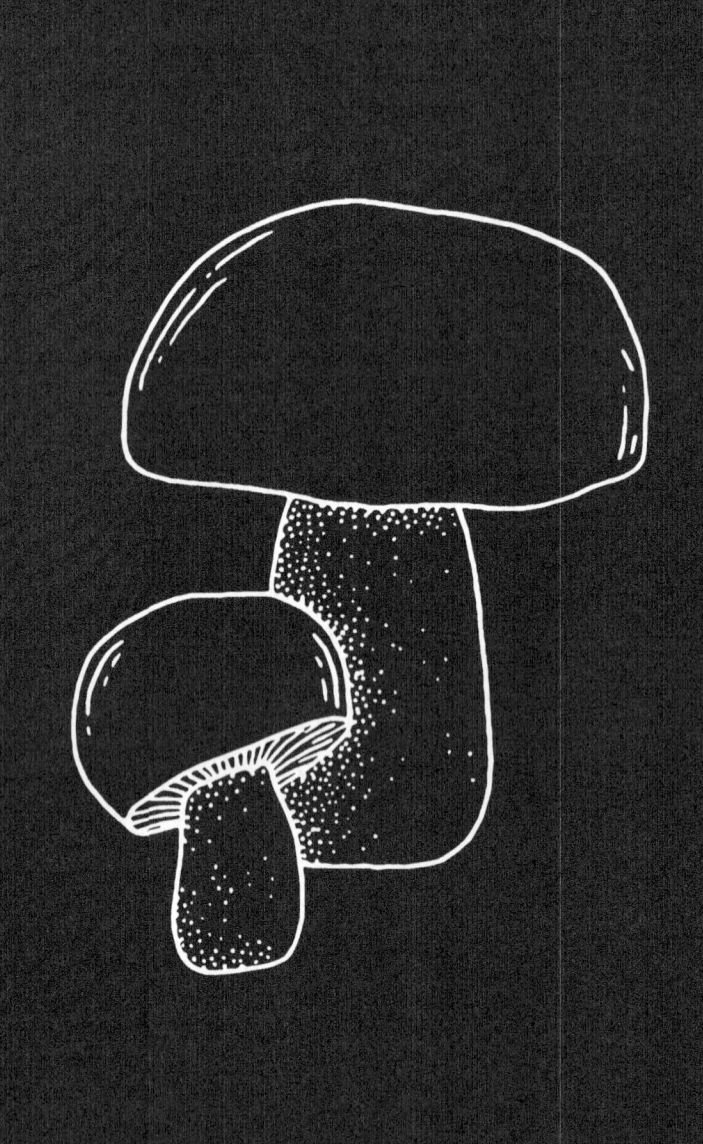

Did you like the book?
Please, leave feedback.

It helps the book stand out
from the crowd.

Printed in Great Britain
by Amazon